Life Hacks
Things I Would Tell My Younger Self

GREG LAURIE

harvest ministries
Riverside, California

LIFE HACKS:
THINGS I WOULD TELL MY YOUNGER SELF

©2025 by Greg Laurie. All rights reserved.

Published by Harvest Ministries

www.harvest.org

Trade paperback ISBN: 978-1-61754-030-1

Unless otherwise indicated, all Scripture quotations are taken from *The New Living Translation*, copyright © 1996, 2004 by Tyndale Charitable Trust. Used by permission of Tyndale House Publishers. All rights reserved.

Scripture quotations marked (NKJV) are taken from: *The Holy Bible, New King James Version* © 1984 by Thomas Nelson, Inc. Scripture quotations marked (NIV) are from The Holy Bible, New International Version®, NIV®. Copyright © 1973, 1978, 1984 by International Bible Society. Used by permission of Zondervan Publishing House.

Scripture quotations marked (TLB) are taken from *The Living Bible*, copyright © 1971 by Tyndale House Publishers, Wheaton, Illinois. Scripture quotations marked (MSG) are taken from The Message, by Eugene Peterson. Copyright © 1993, 1994, 1995, 1996, 2000, 2001, 2002. Used by permission of NavPress Publishing Group. All rights reserved.

Scripture quotations marked (PHILLIPS) are from *The New Testament in Modern English*, Revised Edition © 1958, 1960, 1972 by J. B. Phillips.

No part of this publication may be reproduced, stored in a retrieval system, or transmitted, in any form or by any means—electronic, mechanical, photocopying, recording, or otherwise—without prior written permission.

Printed in the United States of America

Cover Design: Brandon Gillette
Interior Design and Production: Brett Burner

Contents

	A CONVERSATION WITH MY YOUNGER SELF....v
ONE	IT'S GOING TO BE OKAY..........................3
TWO	PUT GOD FIRST IN YOUR LIFE 15
THREE	READ YOUR BIBLE EVERY DAY 21
FOUR	STOP WORRYING AND START PRAYING........25
FIVE	HAVE AN ATTITUDE OF GRATITUDE 29
SIX	LIVE WITH HONESTY AND INTEGRITY........33
SEVEN	MARRY THE RIGHT PERSON 37
EIGHT	SAY "I LOVE YOU" TO THOSE YOU LOVE 41
NINE	KEEP SHORT ACCOUNTS.......................45
TEN	BE A POSITIVE PERSON........................49
ELEVEN	HAVE FUN 53
TWELVE	MAKE GOOD CHOICES..........................59
THIRTEEN	TELL OTHERS ABOUT JESUS 63
FOURTEEN	FINISH YOUR RACE 67
	OTHER BOOKS BY GREG LAURIE.............73

A CONVERSATION WITH MY YOUNGER SELF

> I have been young and now I am old.
> And in all my years I have never seen
> the Lord forsake a man who loves him.
>
> Psalm 37:25 TLB

Imagine for a moment that you had the ability to travel through time.

Are you with me?

Just for a moment, picture what it would be like to actually spend a few hours with your younger self. You track down that earlier version of you (it wouldn't be hard—you know where all your old stomping grounds are) and introduce yourself. Imagine taking a walk on the beach together, sitting on a park bench—or maybe going out for coffee.

What would you say to him—or her?

Would you have some encouragement to share? Would you give your younger self some cautions—or maybe strong warnings? And would your younger self listen to you, or blow off your words? Would you be a good listener, if that younger you just wanted to pour out his or her heart to you?

I've actually spent some time thinking about this.

What would I say to the little lost boy, living with a mother who drank too much and had gone through seven husbands? What words would I share with a Greg Laurie just entering high school—or maybe the newly married Greg, or the one who was just entering the ministry? What advice would I give myself? What things would I tell young Greg to avoid? What things would I challenge young Greg to do better?

A FEW OBVIOUS THINGS

Okay, I know it sounds trivial, but I would probably tell young Greg to floss and brush his teeth every day, because I *know* he wouldn't want to spend as much time at the dentist as the older Greg has.

I would strongly counsel him to get up close and personal with sunscreen every time he went to the beach (which was almost every day). I would remind him that he is a blonde kid, that he burns easily, and that he really doesn't want to visit the dermatologist as many times as the older Greg has had to.

Maybe I would say to a young Greg, "Hey, when all those Star Wars figurines hit the stores after the movies, buy a bunch of them—and leave them in the original packaging, please, because those will turn into valuable collector's items that could send your kids AND grandkids to college."

I would also warn him that he would have his heart broken by a few girls he thought he was in love with, but it would all be worth it because the right girl was coming.

For sure I would tell him to enjoy that nice surfer blonde hair with an excellent wave while he still has it.

That would be my incidental advice. But there are a lot more important things than great teeth and skin and making a few bucks. And if I could take the young Greg Laurie out for coffee—or better yet, In-N-Out—I would open my heart and talk to him about things that would make all the difference in his life—and in his eternity.

Maybe you are reading this little book right now and you don't have the kind of relationship with your dad or mom where you can really talk about the most important issues in life. Maybe, just for these few pages, I could be a dad (or a grandfather) and say things to you that need to be said to a younger person.

Think of these as "life hacks."

My first word of counsel might surprise you, but this is where I would actually start with that young Greg Laurie.

HACKING YOUR LIFE

If you could talk to your younger self, what kind of insights would you tell yourself?

Life Hacks: Things I Would Tell My Younger Self

one

IT'S GOING TO BE OKAY

> The Lord keeps you from all harm
> and watches over your life.
> The Lord keeps watch over you as you come and go,
> both now and forever.
>
> Psalm 121:7-8

Believe it or not, I remember what it was like to be young.

You are experiencing some pretty intense things for the first time. You probably find yourself facing all kinds of choices. People keep asking you about your "plans," but nothing has taken shape yet, and you don't know what to say. You wonder about what you will do with your life, who you will marry, or what career path you might end up on. With the prices of everything these days, maybe you're wondering if you will have to live with your parents into your 20s—or end up on the streets.

You are thinking (maybe worrying) about these things, and then—out of nowhere—something bad happens to you. You have a huge setback. Maybe you break up with your girlfriend or boyfriend, and it almost seems like your world is ending.

So here is what I want to tell you... It's going to be okay. I don't say that lightly; I mean it. You will get through this.

Just recently I came across some really old photos of myself when I was a little boy in New Jersey. I was around six or seven years old. I look at the little guy in that picture, and I know how much suffering he was about to go through. His mother would effectively abandon him. He would never have a father growing up, and would be passed around to various aunts, uncles, and grandparents. He would spend a considerable chunk of his lonely young life in a military school he didn't want to be in.

Sometimes he would be up all night—pulling back the curtain and looking through the dark window—wondering when his mother would come home. Then, when she didn't come home at all, he would have to figure out breakfast and how to get himself ready for school. It was a lot of responsibility for a young boy. I look at those pictures, and my heart aches for him.

But here is what I would tell him. And you.

God has His hand on you. He really does. He will watch over your life. No, it doesn't mean that everything will be easy or fall together like a Hallmark movie. But if you put your life into God's hands, He will walk with you and get you through life—even when life has become very messy and difficult. In the book of Proverbs we find this strong promise:

> Trust in the Lord with all your heart;
> do not depend on your own understanding.
> Seek his will in all you do,
> and he will show you which path to take.
>
> Proverbs 3:5-6

THE PICTURE BY THE FURNACE

Even before young Greg knew about the Lord, God was still helping him and directing his footsteps. During some of those confusing years with a here-and-gone-again mother, I spent a chunk of time living with my grandparents. Looking back, that was probably one of the most stable times in my young life, because they functioned as the parents I'd never had. Both of them were up there in years and were actually born in another century (I'm talking about the 1800s here!). They still believed in old-fashioned values that I didn't understand very well at the time. Fortunately, they also believed in old-fashioned food, too, and I had never eaten like that in my life.

Before I moved in with them, the only hot meals I knew about were called "TV dinners." (Have you heard of those? I think frozen food has come a long way in the last few decades.) So when I landed at my grandparents, I went from food straight out of the freezer to food that had never seen a freezer. My grandmother made everything from scratch, starting with her signature fried chicken.

About that chicken....

In those days, we didn't go to the meat section in the market and buy a chicken all cut up nice and wrapped in plastic. No, on some occasions we started with an actual live chicken. My grandfather would catch one of the birds, lay it across a tree stump, and chop off its head with a hatchet. It freaked me out a little to see the headless chicken running around before it finally flopped down. It wasn't exactly Chick-fil-A, but that was step one in our chicken dinner.

I'd never tasted anything like this food: (very) fresh chicken, mashed potatoes made from scratch, chicken gravy, black-eyed peas, okra and so many other things my grandmother would put on the table every night. Her crowning achievement, however, was her homemade biscuits. With melting butter and blackberry preserves—well, I hope we eat that well in Heaven.

Best of all, it was a stable home. I knew where my grandfather and grandmother would be every night. I knew that when I woke up in the morning, they would be there. The fragrance of freshly brewed coffee and frying bacon and eggs would drift into my room from the kitchen.

In the evenings, we would watch TV together. Each of them had a La-Z-Boy recliner, and I would sit on a little stool between them. Besides watching *I Love Lucy*,

Bonanza, and *Gunsmoke,* I remember so clearly watching this one preacher, who always seemed to be standing in front of these gigantic crowds. I learned that his name was Billy Graham, and I liked him. Little did I know that I would one day have the opportunity to meet him and actually become friends with him.

My grandparents also had a little painting of the face of Jesus over the furnace. It was a floor furnace, and I remember looking at that picture of Jesus for hours, thinking about Him, wondering about Him. In the picture He looked very serious. There was a soft light on His face, and He seemed to be looking off into space. But there was something about Him that interested me and drew me—just like the words of that preacher, Billy Graham. I had no clue at that point that I would come into a relationship with Him, that He would become my best Friend, and that He would change my life forever.

So despite the hardships I went through as a little boy and a young teenager, God had my feet on a path—and that path was leading toward Him. But the road wouldn't be easy.

The fact is, you and I don't get to decide what hand we will be dealt in life.

Maybe you were raised in a stable home, with both a mom and a dad, and some fun family times. Or maybe you live in a broken home, as I did, and you are facing an uncertain future with a lot of anxiety, and maybe even some resentment on your heart. For the most part, you don't get to pick what your life circumstances will be—and neither do I. But you do have the power to decide how you will *respond* to those circumstances.

And here's the thing you will discover in time, no matter how bad your upbringing has been or how many painful experiences you have had to endure. *God can turn your pain into gain.* The mighty Creator of the universe has unlimited power. He can take your setbacks and turn them into set-ups—circumstances that will help you and strengthen you. And even bring you joy. Your tests can become a testimony that you will share with others, as I am doing right now. The troubles you have gone through—and may still be going through—were not designed to destroy you but to develop you. The God who loves you will shape you into a better, stronger, happier version of yourself.

I read recently that Generation Z—those born between 1997 and 2012—have deep fears about the future. At least one third of the young men and women in this generation have had suicidal thoughts, contemplating taking their own lives.

Maybe you have walked through some dark places and had thoughts like that. Maybe the future looks pretty bleak to you right now. Perhaps you have felt like the walls are closing in on you, and the emotional pain you feel is so great that you're not sure you want to live anymore.

I understand that. I have known that kind of darkness and despair at times in my life. But in the year I turned 17,

I began to learn some truths—amazing, incredible truths—that changed my whole outlook.

I learned that my life mattered. Yours does, too.

I learned that I was wanted. You are, too.

I learned that God actually had a special plan for my life—beyond anything I could have dreamed or imagined. And He has a plan like that for you, too. He really, truly does.

A CHANGE IN DIRECTION

I don't know what trajectory your life is on right now. I don't know about the wrong turns you may have taken or the bad decisions you may have made. But I do know this. It is never too late to change. You might think or believe that it is. Other people might tell you that it is. But it's a lie. It's never too late to find a new path. And your first step on that new path can happen today.

I'm not talking here about a change of mind or change of opinion. I'm talking about Someone with all the power in the universe to change the whole course of your life.

It can happen, if you want it to.

It happened to me.

Jesus Christ can literally change the direction of your life, if you will let Him. Your friends may not like it. Your family may not like it. For sure, there is a being called Satan who won't like it at all and will try every trick in the book to turn you away from Jesus. Just as there is a God in Heaven who loves you, there is a devil that's headed for Hell who hates you.

Jesus Himself summed up that contrast in the Bible.

"I am the Gate for the sheep.... All others who came before me were thieves and robbers. But the true sheep did not listen to them. Yes, I am the Gate. Those who come in by way of the Gate will be saved and will go in and out and find green pastures. The thief's purpose is to steal, kill and destroy. My purpose is to give life in all its fullness" (John 10:7-10 TLB).

Sometimes people are apprehensive about giving their life to Jesus, because they imagine that it will involve a bunch of rules, regulations, boredom and misery. Far from it. On the contrary, God's plan for you is better than anything you could plan for yourself if you had a million years to do it. (Doesn't that make sense? He is the one who put you together in the first place.)

God Himself says in Jeremiah 29:11, "For I know the thoughts that I think toward you, says the Lord, thoughts of peace and not of evil, to give you a future and a hope" (NKJV).

Notice that God says, " I know the thoughts that I think toward you."

If that verse had said (God speaking), "I know the single thought I once had about you," I would be happy. But God says, "Thoughts," not " a thought." God is thinking about you all the time.

On my last birthday, my granddaughter Allie wrote this to me on a card—

> "Dear Papa, I Love You and Hope you have a good birthday. You are the best papa in the whole world. You are so nice and you think about me a lot! I Love you!"

That's an unusual thing to say. You might have expected her to write "I think about you a lot" but instead she told me that she knew that I, her grandfather, think about her a lot. To me, that is really the ultimate compliment.

I want you to know God is thinking about you as well. The psalmist says, "How precious are your thoughts about me, O God. They cannot be numbered!" (Psalm 139:17).

You might ask, "But what kind of thoughts is God thinking about me? Negative thoughts? No, they are thoughts of love. And they are also thoughts about your future. God has been with you in your past, He is with you right now in your present, and He will be with you in your future. The Bible says, "Jesus Christ is the same yesterday, today, and forever" (Hebrews 13:8).

Let me pause right here and ask you a couple of very important questions. *Would you like to fill that hole inside of your heart? Would you like to have all of your sins forgiven? Would you like to have a relationship with the God who is thinking of you and your well-being? Would you like to have a fresh start right here, RIGHT NOW?*

Here's what you need to do. You need to realize that God loves you so much that 2,000 years ago He sent His Son Jesus Christ to die on the cross for you. If you will turn from your sin and put your faith in Him, He will come into your life and change you from the inside out—just as He did for me. In that same instant, He will change your eternal destination from Hell to Heaven. You will never have to fear death or being alone again. Ever.

Why don't you just pray this prayer with me? Just pray, *Lord Jesus. I know I am a sinner, and I know You are the Savior. I need You in my life. Forgive me of all of my sin. I choose to follow You from this moment forward. Thank You for hearing this prayer. In Your name, the name of Jesus I pray, Amen.*

So that's the first thing I would say to my younger self.

There is hope, and there is a bright future for you, because of Jesus.

Hold on. Hang in there. It's going to be okay. Whatever you're going through, you will get through it. And you will have the strongest force within you to make sure you do.

HACKING YOUR LIFE

What would you tell yourself right now
about giving yourself to Jesus?

two

PUT GOD FIRST IN YOUR LIFE

> Give your entire attention to what God is doing right now,
> and don't get worked up about what may
> or may not happen tomorrow.
> God will help you deal with whatever hard things
> come up when the time comes.
>
> Matthew 6:34 MSG

This is the second thing I would tell my younger self.

"Greg," I would say, "you need to put God first in your life, no matter what."

This of course starts with asking Christ to come into your life, then it means following Him. Jesus summed it up this way in Matthew 6:33: "But seek first the kingdom of God and His righteousness, and all these things shall be added to you" (NKJV).

"All these things"? All what things? If I was trying to make the point to young Greg, I would explain that Jesus is speaking about more than material things here.

We tend to get obsessed with all of our needs and wants, and we ask ourselves, "Where will I live? What will I do for a job? What kind of car will I drive? Who will go out with me or who should I marry?" These are natural things we think about, and they aren't bad in themselves. But Jesus is saying *don't make those the focus of your life.* Put God first in your thoughts and plans. Seek first the kingdom of God—which means the rule and reign of Christ in your life.

Another way of saying it is put Jesus first. Think about God's will before you consider anything else. When you make decisions, don't put money first, or career first, or politics first, or other people's opinions of you first. Don't even put ministry first. Put Jesus first and He will take care of you and your life.

The Bible tells the story of a young king named Solomon, the son of King David. After David died, the Lord came to Solomon one night in a dream and said, "Ask Me for anything you want, and I will give it to you."

Can you imagine? Here is God, the all-powerful Creator of the universe, offering this young king—maybe 20 to 25 years old—*anything his heart desired.* It's the only place in the Bible where God hands a human being a blank check and says, "Put in whatever amount you want." It was like winning a lottery with no limits at all.

But listen to Solomon's reply:

"O Lord my God, now you have made me the king instead of my father David, but I am as a little child who doesn't know his way around. And here I am among your own chosen people, a nation so great that there are almost too many people to count! Give me an understanding mind so that I can govern your people well and know the difference between what is right and what is wrong. For who by himself is able to carry such a heavy responsibility?" (1 Kings 3:7-9 TLB).

The Bible tells us that God was very pleased with Solomon's answer. And He did just what the young man wanted. He gave the king more wisdom than anyone had ever had—or maybe ever will have. But because Solomon didn't ask for money or palaces or power, He also gave all those things to him as well.

It's a perfect illustration of why putting God first is the right thing to do. No, it doesn't mean that God will make you wealthy or famous. But it does mean that if you put Him first in your life, *everything else will fall into place.* You will have that wonderful sense of your life coming into the right alignment. As the apostle Paul tells us, "This same God who takes care of me will supply all your needs from his glorious riches, which have been given to us in Christ Jesus" (Philippians 4:19).

I can imagine a younger version of Greg looking at me and saying, "What is this 'will of God' thing you keep talking about? How am I supposed to know what God wills for my life?" Here's the answer: You learn the will of God by reading the Word of God. You will begin to understand why God created you, and what His purpose for you might be.

This answers one of the biggest questions you and I will ever have: Why am I here and what is the meaning of my life?

Here's the answer. *You are here to bring glory to God, not to bring glory to yourself.* In Isaiah 43:7, God speaks of "Everyone who is called by My name, Whom I have created for My glory; I have formed him, yes, I have made him" (NKJV).

That is why you are here. God wants to know you and speak to you. God wants to fill you with His Holy Spirit who will guide your steps, speak to you in the night, and be your Companion when all your other friends have slipped out the back door.

Put God first in your life and all the rest of it will be blessed.

HACKING YOUR LIFE

What would you tell yourself about
putting God first in your life?

three

READ YOUR BIBLE EVERY DAY

For the word of God is alive and powerful.
It is sharper than the sharpest two-edged sword,
cutting between soul and spirit, between joint and marrow.
It exposes our innermost thoughts and desires.

Hebrews 4:12

This is one of the main things I would remind young Greg to do. But since the age of 17, he has pretty much done it anyway.

Sometimes I think that as Christians grow in their faith they start to think they don't need to read the Bible as much as they used to. But that's a big mistake. We need to read the Bible every day. You should start the day with it. You should end the day with it.

David put it like this:

"Oh, the joys of those who do not follow evil men's advice, who do not hang around with sinners, scoffing at the things of God. But they delight in doing everything God wants them to, and day and night are always meditating on his laws and thinking about ways to follow him more closely."

Then he goes on to say: "They are like trees along a riverbank bearing luscious fruit each season without fail. Their leaves shall never wither, and all they do shall prosper" (Psalm 1:1-3 TLB).

It couldn't be more clear. If you want to be a happy man or a happy woman, you need to read and think about—or meditate—on the Word of God. In Eastern meditation a person seeks to *empty* their mind, but with biblical meditation one *fills* their mind with the Word of God.

This is how you will grow spiritually. This is how you will be able to resist temptation and keep your feet away from destructive paths. Again, in Psalms, we are told, "How can a young person stay on the path of purity? By living according to your word...I have hidden your word in my heart that I might not sin against you" (Psalm 119:9, 11 NIV).

Please hear me on this: *Success or failure in the Christian life depends on how much of the Bible you get into your life on a regular basis, and how obedient you are to it.*

Read the Word. Treasure the Word. Memorize the Word. In all my life, in all of my travels, I have never met a strong Christian who is not full of Scripture. You never move beyond this any more than you overcome your need to eat, drink, and breathe.

You don't hear someone say, "Oh I used to be into the whole "eating thing" but I don't need food anymore!" Nor do you hear, "I used to breathe with the best of them, but that is in the past!"

Then you will not live much longer. The Word of God in a Christian's life is like eating and breathing. You cannot move forward spiritually without it.

HACKING YOUR LIFE

What would you tell yourself about
reading your Bible every day?

four

STOP WORRYING AND START PRAYING

*Don't worry about anything; instead, pray about everything.
Tell God what you need, and thank him for all he has done.
Then you will experience God's peace,
which exceeds anything we can understand.
His peace will guard your hearts and minds
as you live in Christ Jesus.*

Philippians 4:6-7

This is a piece of advice I could give myself every day. The younger Greg needed to hear it. So does the older Greg.

We all have things to worry about in life. Worry can ruin your day. It can ruin your week. It can ruin your month. Actually, worry can ruin your life. The word *worry* comes from a root word that means to choke or to strangle.

That's what worry does. It chokes you. When you worry about the future, you cripple yourself in the present. Corrie Ten Boom had it right when she said, "Worry does not empty tomorrow of its sorrow, it empties today of its strength."

Jesus said, "So don't be anxious about tomorrow. God will take care of your tomorrow too. Live one day at a time" (Matthew 6:34 TLB). In other words, take each worry and turn it into prayer.

I would compare this to a conditioned reflex. Here's what I mean. Even a little child learns to pull their hand back when they touch a hot stove. That's a natural reflex. A conditioned reflex, however, is something I am *taught* to do. It doesn't come naturally.

It's like when we learn how to drive. When you first begin, you have to consciously think about everything—even using the turn signal. But when I drive now, I don't really think about it at all. I just do it. It's almost automatic.

It should be the same way when you find worry or anxiety welling up in your life and beginning to choke you. When the panic comes, you say, "I'm going to stop everything for a moment and pray. I'm going to ask for His help and guidance." You don't have to find a church and get on your knees or make a big deal about it. You just send up a silent prayer to the Lord, asking for His immediate help, guidance, strength, or perspective.

In 1 Peter 5:7 we read these words: "Cast all your anxiety on him because he cares for you" (NIV). Another translation says it like this: "Let him have all your worries and cares, for he is always thinking about you and watching everything that concerns you" (TLB).

The original language gives us a picture of a definite act of our will where we deliberately choose to stop worrying, and let God assume the responsibility for our welfare.

Years ago, the late Billy Graham was asked this question in an interview: "If you had your life to live over, what would you do differently?"

Billy responded: "I would study more. I would pray more. I would travel less, and take less speaking engagements. If I had it to do all over again, I would spend more time in meditation and prayer, just telling the Lord how much I love and adore Him and looking forward to the time where I will spend with Him for all eternity."

Billy Graham is in that time now. He is in Heaven. I am moved by the fact that he doesn't say he would do more or preach more, if he could live his life again. He says that he would spend more time in God's presence.

That's really good counsel.

The younger Greg needed to hear that advice. And so does the older version.

Hacking Your Life

How would you tell yourself to
stop worrying and start praying?

five

HAVE AN ATTITUDE OF GRATITUDE

> Don't be weary in prayer; keep at it;
> watch for God's answers,
> and remember to be thankful when they come.
>
> Colossians 4:2 TLB

There are circumstances in life that happen to us—*all* of us—that make that make no sense at all. Bad things really do happen to good people. Sometimes bad things even happen to *godly* people.

Take Job as an example. This was a man who was so godly that the Lord was actually bragging on him in Heaven, before Satan and all the angels. It's amazing that we get to listen in on a conversation that took place in Heaven, but the Word of God makes that possible. Here is what God said to Satan: "Have you noticed my servant Job? He is the finest man in all the earth—a good man who fears God and will have nothing to do with evil" (Job 1:8 TLB).

And Satan replied, in effect, "Oh really....?"

The evil one went on to ask God for permission to test Job to the maximum, and God gave him the green light. It makes me think, "I hope God isn't bragging on me. I don't think I could handle the testing the way Job did."

The Lord allowed a series of calamities to both befall his servant in very short order, and Job lost pretty much everything—including his family, his possessions, his reputation, and his health.

And how did he respond? How would *you* respond?

We read that Job gave thanks to God, not for what was happening, but despite what was happening. Here is what he said: "I came naked from my mother's womb...and I shall have nothing when I die. The Lord gave me everything I had, and they were his to take away. Blessed be the name of the Lord" (Job 1:21 TLB).

Job gave thanks to the Lord, and so should we. We might find ourselves saying, "Lord I don't know why this is happening, but I am rejoicing that You are still on the throne. I give thanks to You because You are good, and You are in control of my life."

The Lord doesn't hold us responsible for understanding why things happen as they do. What He asks for is our trust and a thankful heart.

And when you think about it, when did complaining

and moaning and kicking ourselves over regrets ever help our situation or make us feel any better?

It doesn't. It can't. But resting in God's strong embrace helps more than anything else. As the prophet Isaiah declared to our Lord, "You will keep in perfect peace all who trust in you, all whose thoughts are fixed on you!" (Isaiah 26:3).

The apostle Paul wrote these words, "Rejoice in the Lord always. Again I will say, rejoice!" (Philippians 4:4 NKJV).

Paul was not sitting on some beach in the Mediterranean when he wrote that, he was in a prison. But Paul is telling us that we can make a choice to rejoice. Studies have revealed that gratitude actually improves your physical health.

I know there are things that are most likely going wrong in your life, but if you would just pause and count your blessings, I am sure you would find a lot to be thankful for. That alone will improve your outlook. The Bible tells us to "Give thanks to the Lord, for He is good! For His mercy endures forever" (Psalm 107:1 NKJV). That verse does not say, "Give thanks unto the Lord when you feel good."

Fact is, we don't always feel good. We are to give thanks because God is good.

Now if God fails to be good, I suppose we can stop giving thanks. But since that will never happen, we need to have an attitude of gratitude.

Hacking Your Life

What might you tell yourself about having an attitude of gratitude?

six

LIVE WITH HONESTY AND INTEGRITY

You may be sure that your sin will catch up with you.

Numbers 32:23 TLB

Here is a life hack I would bring up with a younger Greg if I had the chance to travel through time and visit with him: Live your life with honesty and integrity.

Integrity is what you are in the dark, when nobody is watching you. Integrity is who you really are as a person, not an image you are projecting to other people.

I would bring this up with my younger self because I have seen such a lack of integrity in our world—back when I was a kid and to this very day. You see people lie, steal, cheat and seem to get away with it. They tell themselves, "Why not? Why should I play by the rules?" People lie and exaggerate on their resumes. They get a contract to build a building even though they cut corners or don't get the proper permits. They cheat on their spouse and never get caught.

Or at least...that's what they imagine. But that is not reality. Everyone gets "caught." Everyone who has ever lived or will live will have to stand before God and give an account of his or her life. So why shouldn't I just go ahead and do "what everyone else is doing"? Because in the end, all these people will have to reap what they sow.

The Bible says, "Do not be deceived, God is not mocked; for whatever a man sows, that he will also reap" (Galatians 6:7 NKJV).

The longer I live, the more impressed I am with character over charisma. I've seen too many preachers with dynamic personalities flameout—or crash and burn—because they didn't seek to maintain honesty and integrity in their lives. That's something I would remind a young Greg, who might have been impressed by people like that.

In the Bible we read of Daniel, a man of integrity who did the right thing throughout all the years of his life. This is one of the few men or women in the Bible without one negative mark against his name.

Having integrity, however, doesn't mean you will always have an easy road. Daniel once found himself under arrest for disobeying the rules of a powerful ruler. The king had issued a decree that no one would be allowed to pray to any god but the king himself (who must have had quite an ego problem.) Daniel, however, prayed anyway. And he didn't do it in the basement behind the furnace. He prayed to his God (as he had always done) before an open window, where everyone could see.

He did this even though he knew the terrible penalty for disobedience—and it wasn't like a parking ticket or a slap on the wrist. Those who were found involved in illegal praying were to be thrown into a den of hungry lions.

That's just what happened to Daniel. But God had the final word. Daniel was protected in that lion's den, but the men who had lied about him were eaten by those same lions.

It is sometimes challenging in this crazy upside-down culture to maintain your integrity in the short term, especially when it seems like those who are dishonest often seem to get ahead. But in the long term you will see, as it is said, "Honesty is the best policy."

Live a life of honesty and integrity. You will be glad you did.

HACKING YOUR LIFE

What would you say to yourself about living with honesty and integrity?

seven

MARRY THE RIGHT PERSON

> Find a good spouse, you find a good life —
> and even more: the favor of God!
>
> Proverbs 18:22 MSG

Her name was Catherine Beatriz Martin, and she became my wife. She was 18, and I was 21.

If you are single, marry the right person! When it comes to important advice and counsel (beyond receiving Jesus as Savior) that pretty much tops the list. And I will have to say that, by the grace of God, the young Greg did very, very well in this department.

I believe God has a person picked out for you. In fact, you can start praying for your spouse-to-be right now. But when you're looking at potential candidates with whom to spend the rest of your life—the person who could be the potential mother or father of your children and the grandparent of your grandchildren—look for a godly person. Look for a person who loves and belongs to Jesus Christ.

Start here: *Find someone who loves the Lord and follows Him even more closely than you do.* Whatever you do, however, don't marry a non-Christian with the thought that you will convert them or change them. Too many sincere men and women have found that path to be a dead end. It is far more likely that they will change you!

The Bible clearly says, "Don't be teamed with those who do not love the Lord, for what do the people of God have in common with the people of sin? How can light live with darkness? And what harmony can there be between Christ and the devil? How can a Christian be a partner with one who doesn't believe?" (2 Corinthians 6:14-15 TLB).

Honestly, marriage is challenging enough. Marrying someone who doesn't share your values and your heart for Jesus will make your life vastly more difficult. Physical intimacy is a wonderful gift of God—but spiritual intimacy will get you through the hard times and dark days. You need someone with whom you can pray, commit things to the Lord, and look to God for strength and wisdom.

Once you make this commitment, however, it should be a *lifelong* commitment. Wedlock should be a padlock—and I mean that in the best way. If you're unwilling to do this, if you want to just experiment with it and get married and then maybe get a divorce "if it doesn't work out," do us all a favor and stay single!

The Bible says, "Love is patient"(1 Corinthians 13:4). That's good to remember. Some people want to rush into marriage. That's never a good idea. Take the time to get to know one another. The Bible says, "Many waters cannot quench love, nor can rivers drown it" (Song of Solomon 8:7). If your love for that man or that woman is a real love, it will stand the test of time.

The late Cliff Barrows gave me a word of advice about marriage that I have never forgotten over breakfast. He said there are eight words you should be willing to say to your spouse every day. Those eight words are: "I'm sorry. Please forgive me. I love you." And I would add four more words: *It was my fault.*

The Bible says, "Each man must love his wife as he loves himself, and the wife must respect her husband" (Ephesians 5:33).

Take your time on this one and seek God's will.

HACKING YOUR LIFE

What would you tell yourself about marrying the right person?

eight

SAY "I LOVE YOU" TO THOSE YOU LOVE

> Most important of all, continue to show
> deep love for each other,
> for love covers a multitude of sins.
>
> 1 Peter 4:8

If I could, I would go back in time to remind myself of this every year—or maybe every day. If you love someone, tell them.

You may say, "Well, they already know that."

Maybe. But it's still good to hear, isn't it?

Please never forget that there will come a moment when you will have a last conversation with someone you love—but you may have no idea that it is the last conversation. That's why it's a good thing to never end a conversation with angry or hurtful words. That's why it's best to end your conversation with "I love you."

The Lord called our son Christopher home when he was only 33 years old. We were devastated beyond words by this horrific event, but this thought gives me comfort: We always told him that we loved him. And he told us he loved us too. He knew that and we reminded him every chance we got. I am very grateful for that.

Don't wait to say loving words at their funeral. They won't hear you. Sure, bring some nice flowers to the memorial service. But why not bring your flowers *now*, and hand them off in person?

Stop for a minute and think about the people closest to you. The people you love. Your parents, your grandparents, your brothers or sisters, your closest friends. Do they know that you love them? How long has it been since you said so? Yes, you could say that in an email or a text, and you probably should. But if you want to really make an impact, *write it on a card* and drop it in the mail. Yes, that may be "old school," but a card is something they can keep. They can put it on a countertop or desk or maybe pull it out now and then and remember what you said. It doesn't have to be a ten-dollar card. It doesn't have to have fancy words or poetry. Maybe all you write is something like this: "I just wanted to take a moment to say that I appreciate you and I love you. Thank you for all that you've done for me."

HACKING YOUR LIFE

What would you tell yourself about saying "I love you" to those you love?

nine

KEEP SHORT ACCOUNTS

> Bear with each other and forgive one another
> if any of you has a grievance against someone.
> Forgive as the Lord forgave you.
>
> Colossians 3:13 NIV

I can see myself sitting down with a younger Greg Laurie, putting a hand on his shoulder, and saying, "Greg, keep short accounts."

In other words, be quick to forgive. Don't keep lists of people's slights or offenses against you. Let's face it, people are going to disappoint you in life—even people you love, admire, and look up to. They can let you down, forget a promise or commitment or say something that hurts you. It will happen. We are all fallible human beings. As James writes, "For we all stumble in many things" (James 3:2 NKJV).

You might feel that you have been betrayed. Maybe you actually have been betrayed. Maybe you just *thought* you were betrayed. But whatever the case, you will face hurt and pain in your life.

Here's what you don't want to do. You don't want to harbor grudges against people, because that can really hurt you—and end up hurting many others as well. Recent studies suggest that those who refuse to forgive are more likely to experience high blood pressure, bouts of depression, and deal with all kinds of anger, stress and anxiety.

By the way, when I forgive someone, I'm not "letting that person off the hook." I am really letting myself off the hook. I am avoiding an untold amount of misery and sadness in my own life. This is not about absolving the perpetrator. It's about healing the victim. And you are the victim if you allow bitterness to overtake you.

In the New Testament book of Hebrews, the author gives this warning: "Watch out that no bitterness takes root among you, for as it springs up it causes deep trouble, hurting many in their spiritual lives" (Hebrews 12:15 TLB). The trouble with holding onto a bitter attitude is that you can't keep it hidden. Sooner or later, it will show itself (and it won't be pretty). It's like the nuclear waste from the 1940s and 1950s that they buried in barrels underground. After a few decades, the barrels began to leak, threatening to contaminate streams and rivers. It's a problem our government has to deal with to this very day.

Don't keep unforgiveness, anger, or bitterness in your heart. Surrender them to Jesus. He will get rid of them forever, and you will be a happier person with a lighter heart.

The man who directs the Stanford Forgiveness Project wrote: "Forgiveness isn't giving in to the other person, it is getting *free* of the other person." Again, when you forgive someone, you set a prisoner free—and that prisoner is yourself.

HACKING YOUR LIFE

What would you say to yourself about keeping short accounts?

ten

BE A POSITIVE PERSON

> Get rid of all bitterness, rage and anger,
> brawling and slander, along with every form of malice.
> Be kind and compassionate to one another.
>
> Ephesians 4:31-32 NIV

It's fine to disagree with someone. Just don't be obnoxious about it.

In the era of social media a new word has been circulating that describes a person who goes on an extended rant.

These people have become known as "Karens." (If your name happens to be Karen, please don't be offended. It's just a snapshot of a current trend.) I don't know how it all started, but when people see a video of someone screaming and yelling, they will sometimes say, "Oh, there goes another *Karen*."

Here is what an older Greg would tell a younger Greg about that kind of activity: *Don't be that person.* As a son or daughter of the living God, you should be known for your love, kindness, and compassion, rather than your anger.

You should be known as an encourager.

You should be known for your kind, helpful words.

You should be known by your family and friends for building people up rather than tearing them down.

You should be known for your self-control, even under stress and pressure.

You should be known for your hopeful, positive outlook on life.

In a room full of depressed, cynical people, you should stand out like a light in the dark place. That's what Jesus meant when He said, "You are the light of the world —like a city on a hilltop that cannot be hidden" (Matthew 5:14).

It's not a matter of trying to do and be all these things; it's simply a matter of letting Jesus shine through your life.

Hacking Your Life

What would you tell yourself about being a positive person?

eleven

HAVE FUN

> Always be full of joy in the Lord.
> I say it again—rejoice!
>
> Philippians 4:4

Would an older Greg really say that to his younger self?

Yes, he would.

You have probably heard this before from the baby boomer generation, but since this is a little book about timely reminders, I will say it again. *Life goes faster the older you grow.* I can't explain it or diagram it but just ask anyone over 50. With every year that goes by, the days seem shorter and shorter. And then one day you look in the mirror and say, "How did *that* happen? When did I suddenly get old?"

Life is short; treasure it. As someone once said, "Enjoy every moment you have, because in life there are no rewinds, only flashbacks." Remember that some of the simplest joys of living are before you every day. Take time to soak in the sunset. Enjoy your meal. Linger a little longer with your family and friends. Don't rush away from the happy times. Don't be in such a hurry to do the next thing.

How do you do that? You might not like my advice.

Put away your smartphone. Don't take it with you to the table. Don't check it every two minutes when you are with other people.

Wherever you are, whomever you are with, BE THERE in that moment.

I love the quote from the martyred missionary, Jim Elliot. He once said, "Wherever you are, be all there! Live to the hilt every situation you believe to be the will of God."

Fortunately, the younger Greg, the one who grew up in the 50s and 60s, didn't have to worry about being distracted by emails, texts, or smartphones. None of those things existed yet (I told you I was old). But there were plenty of other distractions to keep me from the best that God had for me.

So listen up, younger self: I have found the greatest joys in life come from a relationship with God and with others. But sometimes we get so wrapped up in what might be happening in the future that we miss what God has provided for us in the moment. We tell ourselves, *When this happens or that happens, then I'm finally going to be so happy. When I get my driver's license...when I get that job...when I take that trip...when I go to college...when I find a girlfriend or boyfriend...when I get married.... When I finally retire. . .* And on it goes.

But when we invest all of our hopes and expectations in future events that may or may not even happen, we miss those in-between moments, where life really happens. We get so psyched about certain upcoming events that we miss the moments, the interactions, and the opportunities that happen before and after the event.

So here is what I would tell that younger Greg Laurie. Savor the moments when you are with family and friends, and when you are alone with the Lord.

Do you know what I mean by "savor"?

The dictionary defines it as "tasting good food or drink and enjoying it completely." It is to "enjoy or appreciate something pleasant completely, especially by dwelling on it."

Even though Christians face many of the same trials and disappointments and sorrows that everyone else on our broken planet faces, our relationship with Jesus Christ makes all the difference. He is with us. He cares for us. He speaks to us in the very center of who we are. He goes before us and behind us. He has secured an unimaginably wonderful future for us in Heaven with Him.

The Bible calls on us to embrace and walk in that joy. Paul the apostle said, "Always be full of joy in the Lord. I say it again—rejoice!" (Philippians 4:4). And where was

Paul when he wrote those words? Was he lying on some golden beach, feeling the trade winds, eating Cheetos and sipping on a peach iced tea? No, he was in chains in a prison—for no good reason.

In spite of those circumstances, he could write "always be full of joy in the Lord" and *mean* it! In other words, lighten up. Don't take yourself so seriously. Criticize less and compliment more. And don't forget how to laugh at silly things—and laugh at yourself while you are at it.

HACKING YOUR LIFE

What would you tell yourself about
being there and having fun?

twelve

MAKE GOOD CHOICES

> Live life, then, with a due sense of responsibility,
> not as men who do not know the meaning
> and purpose of life but as those who do.
> Make the best use of your time,
> despite all the difficulties of these days.
> Don't be vague but firmly grasp
> what you know to be the will of God.
>
> Ephesians 5:15-17 Phillips

At the beginning of this book, I imagined traveling back in time to visit with a young Greg Laurie. I pictured us walking on the beach together, maybe late in the afternoon, and talking about life.

Well, maybe as our time together is drawing to a close, young Greg, the beach rat, says something like, "Well, this has been cool Mr. Laurie—er, Greg—but it's getting dark and I have to split."

"All right," I might answer, "but I've got just a couple of things left to tell you. I'll make it quick."

"Okay."

"Here is one of the most important things I want you to remember. Make good choices, Greg!"

It's true for all of us. You have a choice each and every day to obey God or to disobey God. To do the right thing or to do the wrong thing. To pick up your Bible and read it or neglect it altogether. To pray or to worry.

These are the sorts of choices that lay before you every day. *Make the right ones.* Why? Because this is the way it works: You make your choices, and then your choices make you. The end of your life is determined by the beginning of your life. The evening of your life is determined by the morning of your life. So if you are young, develop good habits now, start doing the right things now, and that will pay great dividends later in life.

HACKING YOUR LIFE

What would you say to yourself about making good choices?

thirteen

TELL OTHERS ABOUT JESUS

> Always be ready to give a defense
> to everyone who asks you a reason
> for the hope that is in you,
> with meekness and fear.
>
> 1 Peter 3:15 NKJV

In April of 1864, a Union army general named John Sedgwick uttered what turned out to be his last words. He actually had no idea they would be his last words, but that's the way it worked out. Looking out at the Confederate troops firing their muskets in the distance, he told a fellow officer, "They couldn't hit an elephant at this distance."

But he was wrong. No sooner were the words out of his mouth than he was struck down by a musket ball from a Confederate sharpshooter.

Last words can be very significant. In Acts 1:8, the Bible gives us Jesus' last words on earth to His disciples.

They had wanted to know about the big concerns of the day. Would Rome finally be thrown out of Israel? Would a new Jewish kingdom emerge?

But Jesus had something else in mind. He wanted to impress His followers with a huge priority, and He used His last words to do it. He essentially said, "Don't concern yourself with dates and times and when the world might end. Here's what I want you to make number one in your lives...."

Jesus said, "But you will receive power when the Holy Spirit comes upon you. And you will be my witnesses, telling people about me everywhere—in Jerusalem, throughout Judea, in Samaria, and to the ends of the earth" (Acts 1:8).

What does this mean to you and me? It means that we look for opportunities to initiate conversations about Christ.

Maybe it means beginning each day with a brief prayer something like this: "Lord, please open a door for me to speak to somebody about You today. And help me to be alert and ready when that door opens."

That's what life in Christ is all about, and I can't imagine a better one. To the best of our ability, we seek to lead people to the Lord, and then we disciple them. In other words, we help new believers get up on their feet spiritually, and we stay available to help and encourage them. That will be an amazing, unforgettable help to them, but it will transform your life as well, bringing you a sense of joy and satisfaction beyond anything you have experienced to that point.

I remember one of my friends telling me about being in a simple Bible study with a new believer. He was explaining a verse to the new Christian when he saw something he had never seen before.

"It was like the shutters lifted and a light went on in his eyes, Greg. *I saw it!* The Lord suddenly showed him something he had never seen before, and his whole face lit up." My friend was so excited about that moment. I can't think of anything to top an experience like that.

Maybe you are the young believer who needs to find an older Christian to walk with for a while. I remember when I was a brand-new Christian at age 17. I knew a lot of Christians my own age, but I remember thinking, "These guys don't know much more than I know!"

So I sought out people like my pastor and his wife, Chuck and Kay Smith. And when they were too busy, I tried to spend time with Pastor Romaine, an associate at the church. I really didn't have the advantage of a mom or dad who cared for me growing up, so I needed time with older Christians who could help me work through some things and untie a few knots in my life. I had meals with them, worked alongside them, did fun things with them, and got to see what a Christian looks like up close and personal.

So if you're a younger believer, ask the Lord to bring an older believer into your life, who can help you to find the best paths and steer you away from the dangerous ones.

HACKING YOUR LIFE

What would you say to yourself about telling others about Jesus?

fourteen

FINISH YOUR RACE

> Don't you realize that in a race everyone runs,
> but only one person gets the prize? So run to win!
> All athletes are disciplined in their training.
> They do it to win a prize that will fade away,
> but we do it for an eternal prize.
> So I run with purpose in every step.
>
> 1 Corinthians 9:24-26

For every one of us, there will come a moment when we have our last meal, speak our last words, and breathe our last breath on this planet.

And then, this race called life will be over.

Yes, for those who belong to Christ, life will go on forever. But life on this earth, in this body, won't. You may imagine that you don't have to think about that for another 50 or 60 years, but we can't know that. Tomorrow might be your last day, or even today. That's not being a downer or gloomy. It's just the way life works on this planet.

The apostle Paul could almost put his departure date on the calendar, because he was in a Roman prison awaiting execution. So in his last letter to his young friend Timothy he wrote, "I have fought the good fight, I have finished the race, and I have remained faithful. And now the prize awaits me" (2 Timothy 4:7-8).

You don't know when the end of your race will come. My son Christopher's race ended at age 33. When he left the house that last morning and got into his car, he had no idea that he had just walked through that door for the final time and said his last goodbyes. Honestly, it still breaks my heart. I of course wish I could have had a final conversation with him, but it was not to be.

Speaking of racing, he and I used to race on the beach as he was growing up. He was a great runner, but somehow—for many years—I managed to beat him.

But when it came to getting to Heaven and seeing the Lord face to face, Christopher beat me there. He has gone to Heaven before me, though no one could have ever expected that.

You may say to yourself, "I still have a long way to run in this race. It's like an ultra-marathon, and I've only gone a few miles. Maybe I'll get right with God when I'm in my 80s or 90s.

That's not a good idea at all. We really have no idea how long our race might be.

I remember asking my mentor, Chuck Smith, what an older Chuck would say to a younger Chuck, if he could talk to him.

"What advice would you give your younger self?" I asked him.

He thought about it for a moment, and then in that distinctive voice of his, he replied, "I would say, 'Hold the course.'"

"Hold the course?" I wasn't sure what he meant.

"Do you mean, just hang in there and keep running?"

His response was, "Yes, hold the course."

And he did. He held the course into his mid-80s before the Lord called him home.

Maybe as you are reading these last couple of pages you are thinking, "It's too late for me. I've made too many bad decisions. I've messed up too many opportunities and hurt too many people. I have known what was right and turned away from it. It's too late for me."

But it's not. Can you handle news that good? It's not!

God can turn your life around. I've seen it happen hundreds—thousands—of times for men and women from every age and background. God can forgive you of your sin. God can refresh you and replenish you and revive you and set you on a new course, but you must turn to Him.

Earlier in this book, I gave an opportunity for someone to come to the Lord for the first time. But maybe your situation is different. Maybe you used to walk with Him but have turned away. Let me do an invitation of a different kind right now to prodigal sons and daughters who have been running from God and trying to forget about Him.

He has not forgotten about you. He loves you. God will accept you, forgive you, and completely restore you. You might wonder, how would God treat me if I returned to Him? *He would forgive you. He would draw you into His embrace.*

After the end of the Civil War, Abraham Lincoln was asked how the Northerners should treat the Southerners who had once broken away from the United States to go their own way. He replied, "Treat them as if they had never left."

That is how God will treat you if you turn back to Him with all your heart. It will be as if you never turned away. When Jesus died on the cross 2,000 years ago and paid the penalty for your sins, it was not a partial payment. He paid it all. It was a complete payment.

Maybe it's time to return to Him.

It's time to come home.

HACKING YOUR LIFE

What would you tell yourself about finishing your race?

OTHER BOOKS BY GREG LAURIE

As It Is in Heaven

FAME: Fortunes, Failure and Faith

Jesus Revolution

Lennon, Dylan, Alice, and Jesus

Revelation: A Book of Promises

Billy Graham: The Man I Knew

World Changers

Bringing Christ into Your Crisis

God's Answer to Fear, Worry, and Anxiety

Hope for Hurting Hearts

Steve McQueen: The Salvation of an American Icon

Johnny Cash: The Redemption of an American Icon

And so many more!

Visit harvest.org

discipleship

Connect with the
Harvest: Discipleship Platform
to fellowship with like-minded believers
and find valuable resources.

Grow with us at:
DISCIPLE.HARVEST.ORG

www.ingramcontent.com/pod-product-compliance
Lightning Source LLC
LaVergne TN
LVHW011206060625
813050LV00020B/129